POSITIVELY Pineapple

Quilts for the Pineapple Rule®…and more

LYNDA MILLIGAN & NANCY SMITH

Book Production

Sharon Holmes — Editor, Technical Illustrator
Susan Johnson — Quilt Designer, Photo Stylist
Lexie Foster — Cover, Quilt, and Graphic Designer
Christine Scott — Editorial Assistant
Sandi Fruehling — Copy Reader
Brad Bartholomew — Photographer

Thanks

Sewing & Quilting — Nancy Smith, Jane Dumler, Ann Petersen, Katie Wells, Sue Williams, Terri Wiley, Christine Scott, Christine Marcum
Long-arm Machine Quilting — Sandi Fruehling, Susan F. Geddes, Kay Morrison, Carolyn Schmitt

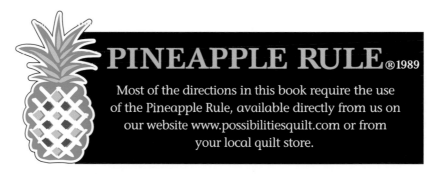

PINEAPPLE RULE ®1989

Most of the directions in this book require the use of the Pineapple Rule, available directly from us on our website www.possibilitiesquilt.com or from your local quilt store.

Every effort has been made to ensure that the information in this book is accurate. Due to individual skills, conditions, and tools, we cannot be responsible for any losses, injuries, or other damages that may result from its use.

POSSIBILITIES ®

Fabric Designers for Avlyn, Inc. • Publishers of Possibilities® Books
Home of Great American Quilt Factory, Inc.
www.greatamericanquilt.com
1-800-464-2665

Positively Pineapple
©2005 Lynda Milligan & Nancy Smith

All rights reserved. No part of this book may be reproduced in any form without permission of the authors. The written instructions, photographs, patterns, and designs are intended for the retail purchaser and are protected under federal copyright laws. Projects may not be manufactured for commercial sale. Published by Possibilities® in Denver, Colorado, USA.

Library of Congress Control Number: 2005906990   ISBN: 1-880972-57-3

Introduction

Our first book on Pineapple quilts was printed in 1989, and we have never lost our enthusiasm for them! Using the Pineapple Rule® makes the blocks easy and fast, with no templates or tearing away of paper required. We know you will enjoy many hours of creative fun making Pineapple quilts.

Organization of Positively Pineapple

Beginning on page 3 is a general directions section for the Pineapple Rule®. Page 6 starts a section of ideas for striking out on your own to explore the endless possibilities of the Pineapple. Many quilting options are shown on page 8, and a handy chart for making basic bed-sized quilts appears on page 9. Be sure to see the Quilters' Gallery on pages 40-43 for even more great ideas.

Positively Pineapple contains detailed directions for thirteen quilts made with the Pineapple Rule®. In addition we have included paper-piecing patterns for 6″ and 2″ blocks which are fun for making small projects. Directions are given for a pin cushion and a pillow which use the 6″ paper-pieced block, and a cute key chain or pin using the 2″ block. We know you will think of many other applications for these patterns! Several of the gallery quilts were made with the 6″ paper-piecing pattern. Full directions for our popular Pineapple place mat are also included.

You may notice that we have included several quilts in this book that are not traditional Pineapples. The reason for this is that the Pineapple Rule® can be used to create many basic units and partial Pineapples, and we just had to share the concept with you! *Strawberries and Cream* is made with a square-in-a-square block—the center of a Pineapple block. It is made quickly with our ruler and the directions for Row 1. *Which Witch?* uses Rows 1 and 2 of the Pineapple Rule® Directions, creating a great frame for a Halloween print. *Jellybeans* is made by adding wider segments at the corners of the block for every even row. The trimming creates a repeating triangle—Flying Geese with the Pineapple Rule®! In addition, the coloration of Jellybeans creates the same effect as the Log Cabin lantern variation, a favorite of ours. We know you will find other ways to use the Pineapple Rule® as you explore the world of Pineapples.

Getting Started

After you have chosen a quilt to make and have purchased the yardage required, you are ready to start!

We recommend washing the fabric to preshrink it and to remove excess dye and manufacturing sizing. Iron each fabric and, if desired, use spray starch for added stability.

The cutting chart for your quilt will tell you to cut strips of different widths. Labeling the stacks of strips at this point is helpful. Step 1 of the directions will tell you to subcut some of the strips into segments to use for specific rows in the construction of the block. From there you will be referred to the Pineapple Rule® Directions starting on page 3 for explicit directions and diagrams for using the ruler to trim the corners of each row as the block grows.

Have fun!

The diagrams below represent the basic blocks for many of the quilts in this book, 8″ and 12″, with two corner options, A and B.

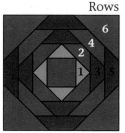

Rows

Quilts with this size block and corner option are:

Twilight- page 20
Provence - page 24
Poppies - page 32

8″ Block • Corner A

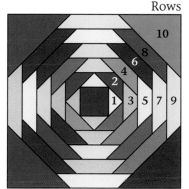

Rows

Quilts with this size block and corner option are:

Bed-Sized Quilts - 9
Barn Dance - 26

12″ Block • Corner A

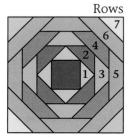

Rows

Quilts with this size block and corner option are:

Bundle of Joy - 14

8″ Block • Corner B

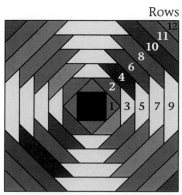

Rows

Quilts with this size block and corner option are:

Mocha Latte - 28

12″ Block • Corner B

Directions for One Block

Use ¼″ seam allowance unless otherwise noted.

Row 1: Mark diagonal lines from corner to corner across wrong side of center square. Stitch Row 1 pieces to opposite sides of center square. Press. Repeat on remaining sides. Carefully press seam allowances toward outside of block; do not stretch square out of shape.

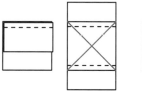

Lay Pineapple Rule® on wrong side of block, **inside diagonal lines on ruler on top of seam lines and center vertical line matching marked center line on center square**. A horizontal line on ruler may not fall exactly on the horizontal pencil line but should be parallel and equidistant from it. Trim off the two triangles of fabric at corner. Repeat at other corners of block.

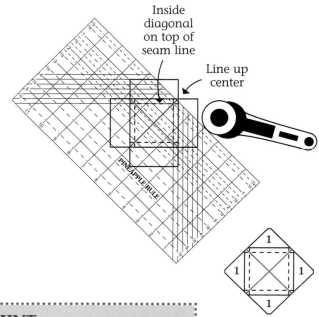

Inside diagonal on top of seam line

Line up center

HINT

To ensure accuracy, complete each row on all blocks as you go. Use the same ruler markings for each row on each block. The position of horizontal and diagonal lines will change as the blocks increase in size, but for each row, use the same set of lines.

Row 2: Stitch Row 2 pieces to block as in Row 1. They will be slightly longer than necessary. Press seam allowances to outside of block. Draw lines from corner to corner, keeping right angle at center. Lay ruler on block as before, **lining up the inside diagonal lines on the seam lines.** Continue to use center and horizontal lines on ruler. Trim corners.

Row 3: Stitch Row 3 pieces to block. Press seam allowances to outside of block, being careful not to stretch the block. Trim the corners, **this time lining up the edge of the ruler with the edge of Row 2.** Continue to use center, horizontal, and diagonal lines on ruler.

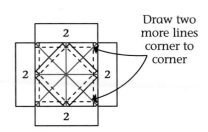

Draw two more lines corner to corner

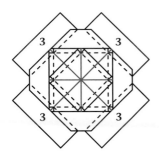

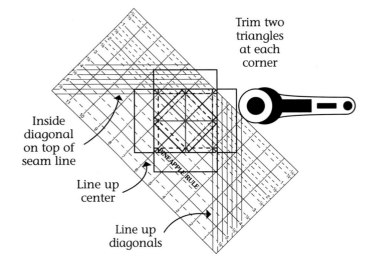

Trim two triangles at each corner

Inside diagonal on top of seam line

Line up center

Line up diagonals

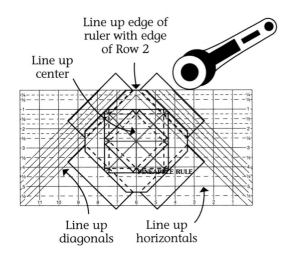

Line up edge of ruler with edge of Row 2

Line up center

Line up diagonals

Line up horizontals

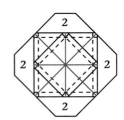

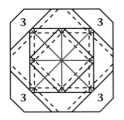

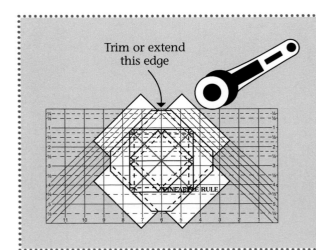

Trim or extend this edge

TROUBLESHOOTING

To match vertical, horizontal, and diagonal lines on ruler to block, you may need to trim or extend an edge. For example, you may have to move the ruler up or down, away from the edge of the previous row, in order to match the lines. This inaccuracy may be due to incorrect seam allowances, excessive pressing, stretching, etc. Trimming or extending an edge is a way to compensate so all blocks remain square and of equal size.

Row 4: Stitch Row 4 pieces to block. To minimize distortion, sew with block on bottom, strip on top. Press as before, being careful not to stretch the block. Trim the corners, **lining up the edge of the ruler with the edge of Row 3** and continuing to use center, horizontal, and diagonal lines.

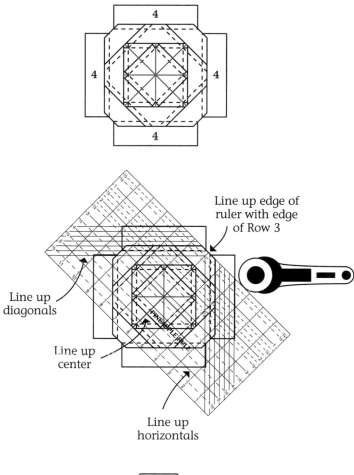

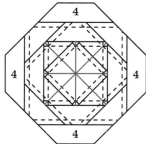

Row 5 (8″ block) or Rows 5-9 (12″ block):
Continue stitching, pressing, and trimming in the same manner as for Row 4.

Corner Rows

This last section is for completing the corners of the block. Corner A is made with wider strips which creates large corner triangles. Corner B, on page 6, is made with several narrow strips. Skip to the directions and diagrams for the block you are making.

Row 6 (8″ Block • Corner A) or Row 10 (12″ Block • Corner A):

Stitch Row 6 or Row 10 pieces to corners of block (corners of block are sewn to Row 4 or Row 8—refer to block diagram for your quilt). Press. Line up one corner of the Pineapple Rule® with two adjacent sides of the block. Trim both sides of the corner without moving the ruler. Repeat on other corners.

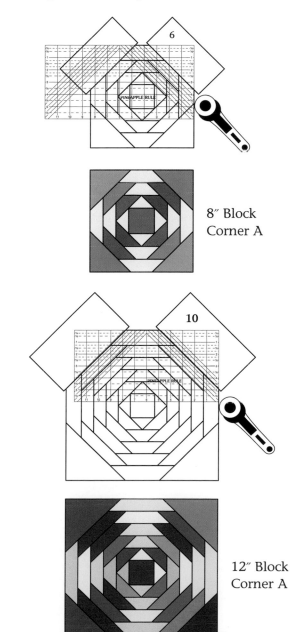

8″ Block
Corner A

12″ Block
Corner A

Rows 6-7
(8″ Block • Corner B)
or Rows 10-12
(12″ Block • Corner B):

Stitch Rows 6-7 or Rows 10-12 to corners of block (corners of block are sewn to Row 4 or Row 8). Press. Line up one corner of the Pineapple Rule® with two adjacent sides of the block. Trim both sides of the corner without moving the ruler. Repeat on other corners.

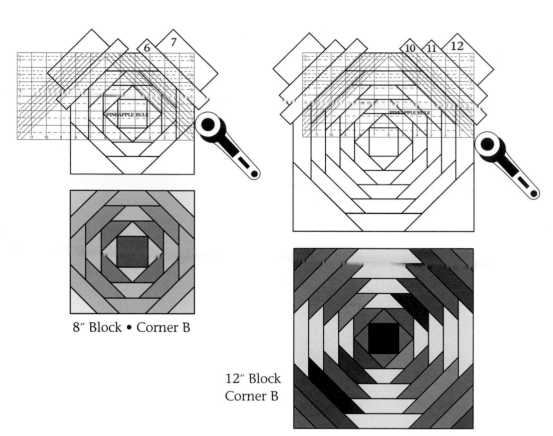

8″ Block • Corner B

12″ Block Corner B

Striking Out on Your Own

Want to try something different in a Pineapple—perhaps experiment with color placement or strip width? Strike out on your own! Here are some ideas to get you started.

Coloring Diagrams & Fabric Pasteups

Make photocopies of the 6″ paper-piecing block on page 39 and color them with pencils, crayons, or markers. If desired, translate them into fabric paste-ups by attaching strips of fabric over the coloring or on new photocopies. Place colored or fabric mockup blocks between upright mirrors as shown in photo at right. Four blocks appear, and without sewing a stitch, you can see how your colors and design will look. The area where the corners of the blocks meet is now visible. There are many ways to vary the corners to make secondary designs where they come together. Try adding a narrow strip, in a contrasting fabric, before the last corner strip, or piece the last strip before adding it to the corner (see diagrams on page 7).

Mirrors can also be used with a stitched block to preview the effectiveness of a design.

Vary Fabric Choices

Try using a stripe, cut either on the crosswise or the lengthwise grain, in your block. Complement large prints with solids or near-solids. Experiment with the addition of a black fabric in your block. Try fussy-cutting a favorite fabric or using a photo transfer as an enlarged block center (see Which Witch? on pages 12-13).

Vary Center Square Strip Width

Another way to change your blocks is to experiment with different sizes of center squares and different strip widths. To use our Pineapple Rule® diagrams, keep a 2:1 ratio of finished center size to finished row widths. For example:

finished center 2½" with finished row 1¼" wide
finished center 3" with finished row 1½" wide
finished center 3½" with finished row 1¾" wide

Center Square on Point

A block can be finished by stitching the corners to the "sides" of the block (adding them to the odd rows rather than the even rows). This rotates the center square a quarter turn (see example below).

Assymetrical Coloration

Coloring the rows of Pineapple blocks in unusual ways can open up whole new worlds of design. You can create something similar to the Amish Blossoms quilt in the Quilter's Gallery, page 41 by making colors flow from one block to another. See the examples below for inspiration, then strike out on your own for hours of creative fun.

Paper Piecing Variations

Paper-pieced Pineapples offer another avenue for producing original designs. The size of the 6″ paper-piecing block on page 39 can be changed by making photocopies at 66% for a 4″ block (outside seam allowance of block must then be adjusted). Take another step and design some of your own patterns. In a block with the rows of two adjacent sides 1″ wide, and the rows of the remaining sides ½" wide, the center square will be off center, and the angles become sharper than the 45° angles in a "normal" block, leading to interesting effects (see Prickly Pineapple in Quilters' Gallery, page 40).

Put a narrow strip near the corner.

Finish the corners so the center square stands on point.

Make assymetrical blocks and rotate them for different effects.

Piece the center square.

Piece the strips used for the corners.

Try different values for the backgrounds of assymetrical blocks.

7

Quilting Ideas

Quilt concentric shapes by quilting in the ditch or ⅛″ to ¼″ away from seams.

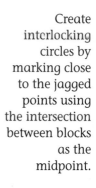

Create interlocking circles by marking close to the jagged points using the intersection between blocks as the midpoint.

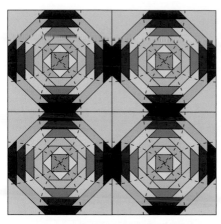

Quilt along each side of the jagged points. Quilt the center squares and the large squares formed by the corners of four blocks.

Quilt down the centers of the strips to accent a design, then add parallel or radiating lines to fill remaining spaces.

Use your favorite floral quilting pattern to center on each block. Applique patterns can be converted into great quilting patterns also.

Quilt diamonds using the jagged points as guides. Fill in with diamonds in the background areas and squares in the centers.

Quilt concentric squares down centers of strips.

Draw circles with a compass or mark around a plate to create interlocking shapes.

Bed-Sized Quilts
12" Block   See Spice Rack, page 42.

Twin, double/queen, and king are "comforter" size—they cover a 12" deep mattress but do not cover the pillows. If your mattress is deeper than 12", adjust border widths accordingly.

Yardage is calculated for one light for odd rows, one dark for even rows, and a third fabric for centers.

Backings are calculated for vertical seams.

After cutting strips for blocks, use small chart at bottom of page to cut strips into segments. Refer to Pineapple Rule® Directions, pages 3-6, for sewing blocks. Refer to Jellybeans, page 46, Steps 3-6, for borders, quilting, and binding.

	BABY 46x58" 12 blocks set 3x4	TWIN 69x93" 24 blocks set 4x6	DBL/QUEEN 90x102" 30 blocks set 5x6	KING 108x96" 42 blocks set 7x6
YARDAGE Choose fabric with 42" usable width.				
Centers	⅙ yd	¼ yd	¼ yd	⅓ yd
Light	1½ yd	2¾ yd	3⅜ yd	4⅝ yd
Dark	2⅝ yd	5 yd	6⅛ yd	8⅜ yd
Border 1	⅓ yd	¾ yd	1 yd	¾ yd
Border 2	¾ yd	1 yd	1½ yd	1⅜ yd
Border 3	—	1⅜ yd	2⅛ yd	2⅛ yd
Binding	⅝ yd	¾ yd	⅞ yd	⅞ yd
Backing	3¾ yd	5⅞ yd	9⅜ yd	8⅞ yd
Batting	50x62"	75x99"	96x108"	114x102"
CUTTING Cut strips from selvage to selvage.				
Centers	1 strip 2½"	2 strips 2½"	2 strips 2½"	3 strips 2½"
Light Rows 1-3-5-7-9	30 strips 1½" wide	60 strips 1½" wide	75 strips 1½" wide	105 strips 1½" wide
Dark Rows 2-4-6-8	27 strips 1½" wide	53 strips 1½" wide	66 strips 1½" wide	93 strips 1½" wide
Row 10	10 strips 4¼" wide	20 strips 4¼" wide	24 strips 4¼" wide	34 strips 4¼" wide
Border 1	5 strips 1½" wide	7 strips 3" wide	8 strips 3½" wide	9 strips 2½" wide
Border 2	5 strips 4½" wide	7 strips 4" wide	8 strips 5½" wide	9 strips 4½" wide
Border 3	—	8 strips 5" wide	9 strips 7½" wide	10 strips 6½" wide
Binding	6 strips 2½" wide	9 strips 2½" wide	10 strips 2½" wide	11 strips 2½" wide

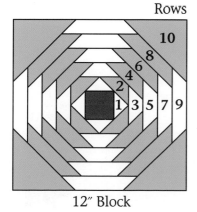

Rows

12" Block

Stack 2½" center strips and cut into 2½" squares. Baby–12 squares, Twin–24 squares, Double/Queen–30 squares, King–42 squares.

Stack 1½" strips of light for Rows 1-3-5-7-9 and cut into segments listed below. Repeat with dark for Rows 2-4-6-8. Baby–48 segments for each row, Twin–96 segments each, Double/Queen–120 segments each, King–168 segments each.

Light		Dark	
Row 1 - 2½" segments		Row 2 - 3½" segments	
Row 3 - 4" segments		Row 4 - 5" segments	
Row 5 - 5" segments		Row 6 - 6" segments	
Row 7 - 6" segments		Row 8 - 6½" segments	
Row 9 - 6½" segments			

Stack 4¼" strips of dark for Row 10 and cut into segments.
Row 10 - 7½" segments

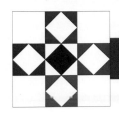

33x33" • 3" Block

This quilt is made with a square-in-a-square block which uses Row 1 of Pineapple Rule® Directions.

Yardage
Choose fabrics with 42" usable width.

Blocks	¼ yd each of 10 reds
	¼ yd each of 10 whites
Border 1	⅓ yd white
Border 2	⅙ yd red
Border 3	⅝ yd white
Binding	⅜ yd
Backing	1⅛ yd
Batting	38x38"

Cutting
Cut strips from selvage to selvage.

Blocks	1 strip 1¾" wide from each fabric
	2-3 squares 2⅝" from each fabric (total of 25 red, 24 white)
	2-3 pieces 2x3½" from each white (total of 28)
	3-4 squares 2" from each red (total of 32)
	2-3 squares 2" from each white (total of 24)
	4 squares 2" - white
Border 1	4 strips 2" wide
Border 2	4 strips ⅞" wide
Border 3	4 strips 3½" wide
Binding	4 strips 2½" wide

Directions
Sew ¼" seams unless otherwise noted.

1. BLOCKS: Stack 1¾" strips and cut into 2⅝" segments—10 pieces from each white, 9-10 pieces from each red. Using 2⅝" squares and 1¾x2⅝" pieces, make 25 blocks with red centers and white corners and 24 blocks with white centers and red corners. Press seam allowances toward the red on both blocks. See Pineapple Rule® Directions, Row 1, page 3, and the diagrams below.

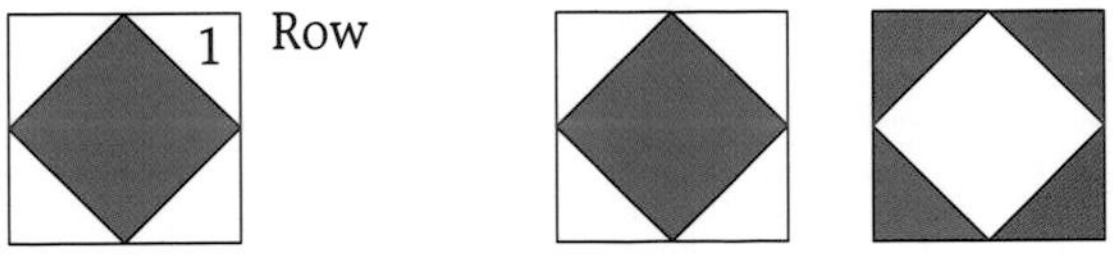

Make 25

Make 24

2. HALF-BLOCKS: Make 16 half-blocks with 2x3½" white pieces and 2" red squares. Press seam allowances toward red. Make 12 half-blocks with 2x3½" white pieces and 2" white squares.

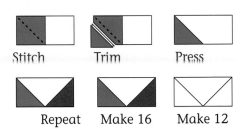

3. ASSEMBLE: Adding 2" white squares as shown, stitch blocks and half-blocks together into horizontal rows. Stitch rows together. Press.

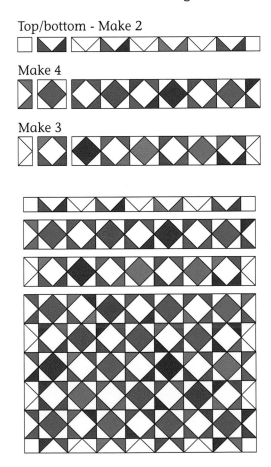

4. BORDER 1: Cut 2 Border 1 strips to fit sides of quilt. Stitch to quilt. Press. Repeat at top and bottom.

Continued on page 45.

10

Place mat pattern on page 36.

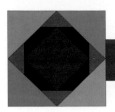

57x74″ • 6″ Block (8½″ with setting triangles)

Rows 1 and 2 of Pineapple Rule® Directions are used to make the block for Which Witch? The large center is a great place to display a favorite fabric or perhaps a photo transfer.

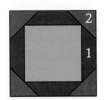

Rows

Yardage
Choose fabrics with 42″ usable width.

Blocks	¾ yd Halloween print (if fussy cutting characters, they should fit in 4″ squares & 2 or more yards of fabric may be needed)
	⅞ yd black
	1⅜ yd black & white check
Setting triangles	⅜ yd each of 7 fabrics yellows & oranges
Border 1	½ yd orange
Border 2	⅓ yd yellow stripe
Border 3	1⅓ yd black
Binding	⅝ yd
Backing	3¾ yd
Batting	63x80″

Cutting
Cut strips from selvage to selvage.

*Cut these squares in **half** diagonally.

Blocks	print	35 squares 4½″
	black	18 strips 1½″ wide - Row 1
	check	18 strips 2¼″ wide - Row 2
Setting triangles		*70 squares 5⅛″ - 10 from each fabric
Border 1		6 strips 2″ wide
Border 2		6 strips 1¼″ wide
Border 3		7 strips 5½″ wide
Binding		7 strips 2½″ wide

Directions
Sew ¼″ seams unless otherwise noted.

1. BLOCKS:

    Stack 1½″ black strips and cut into segments

Row 1	4½″ segments	140 pieces

    Stack 2¼″ black check strips and cut into segments.

Row 2	4½″ segments	140 pieces

    Make 35 blocks. See Pineapple Rule® Directions, pages 3-4. Only Rows 1 and 2 are needed.

2. SETTING TRIANGLES: Add 4 setting triangles of the same fabric to sides of block. Press. Repeat with remaining blocks.

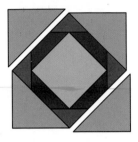

3. ASSEMBLE: Stitch blocks together into horizontal rows. Stitch rows together. Press.

Continued on page 44.

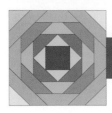

Bundle of Joy

39 x 47" • 8" Block Corner B

The blocks for this quilt are identical, made with shaded pinks and greens or blues and greens.

Yardage
Choose fabrics with 42" usable width.
See page 44 for yardage chart for blue version.

Block   ¼ yd dark pink - centers
       ½ yd medium dark pink - Row 2
       ⅝ yd medium pink - Row 4
       ¾ yd medium light pink - Row 6
       ⅓ yd each of 2 light pinks - Row 7
       ⅓ yd light green - Row 1
       ½ yd medium light green - Row 3
       ⅝ yd medium green - Row 5

Border 1   ¼ yd
Border 2   ⅝ yd
Binding   ½ yd
Backing   1½ yd
Batting   43 x 51"

Cutting
Cut strips from selvage to selvage.

Block   dk pink   20 squares 2½" - centers
       lt green   5 strips 1½" wide - Row 1
       med lt green   8 strips 1½" wide - Row 3
       med green   10 strips 1½" wide - Row 5
       med dk pink   8 strips 1½" wide - Row 2
       med pink   10 strips 1½" wide - Row 4
       med lt pink   14 strips 1½" wide - Row 6
       lt pink #1   4 strips 2¼" wide - Row 7
       lt pink #2   4 strips 2¼" wide - Row 7

Border 1   4 strips 1" wide
Border 2   4-5 strips 3½" wide
Binding   5 strips 2½" wide

Directions
Sew ¼" seams unless otherwise noted.

1. BLOCKS:

Cut 1½" green strips into segments:
    Row 1   2½" segments   80 pieces
    Row 3   4" segments   80 pieces
    Row 5   5" segments   80 pieces

Cut 1½" pink strips into segments:
    Row 2   3½" segments   80 pieces
    Row 4   5" segments   80 pieces
    Row 6   6" segments   80 pieces

Cut 2¼" pink strips into segments:
    Row 7   4" segments   40 pieces each fabric

Make 20 blocks. See Pineapple Rule® Directions, pages 3-6. For Row 7, use one pink on opposite corners and second pink on remaining opposite corners.

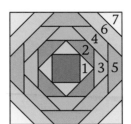

Rows

2. ASSEMBLE: Stitch blocks together into horizontal rows. Stitch rows together. Press.

3. BORDERS: Cut Border 1 strips to fit sides of quilt. Stitch to quilt. Press. Repeat at top and bottom. Repeat for Border 2, piecing strips end to end if necessary.

Continued on page 44.

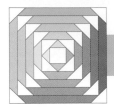

Jellybeans

62 x 74″ • 12″ Block

This block is made using directions for Rows 1-3 of Pineapple Rule® Directions, creating the repeating white triangles in the corners.

Yardage
Choose fabrics with 42″ usable width.

Blocks	¼ yd each of 5 oranges
	¼ yd each of 5 pinks
	¼ yd each of 5 yellows
	¼ yd each of 5 greens

Blocks, Borders 1, 3	4⅞ yd white
Border 2	⅜ yd
Binding	⅝ yd
Backing	4⅛ yd
Batting	68 x 80″

Cutting
Cut strips from selvage to selvage.

Blocks	4 strips 1½″ wide from each fabric
White	20 squares 2½″ (from 2 strips 2½″ wide)
	45 strips 2½″ wide - blocks
	6 strips 2½″ wide - Border 1
	7 strips 4½″ wide - Border 3
Border 2	6 strips 1½″ wide
Binding	7 strips 2½″ wide

Directions
Sew ¼″ seams unless otherwise noted.

1. BLOCKS:
   Stack 1½″ strips and cut into segments.

Row 1	2½″ segments	4 of each fabric
Row 3	4½″ segments	4 of each fabric
Row 5	6½″ segments	4 of each fabric
Row 7	8½″ segments	4 of each fabric
Row 9	10½″ segments	4 of each fabric

   Stack 2½″ white strips and cut into segments.

   | Rows 2, 4, 6, 8, 10 | 4½″ segments | 442 pieces |

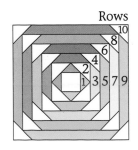

Rows

Make 20 blocks. Use fabrics in positions desired, but arrange colors as shown in block diagram. See Pineapple Rule® Directions, pages 3-4. **Use diagrams for Row 1.** Every **even** row of Jellybeans uses the inside diagonal lines on the ruler and creates a white triangle on the corner. **Use diagrams for Row 2 for every even row. Use diagrams for Row 3 for odd rows 3-9.** See also the diagrams below.

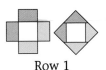

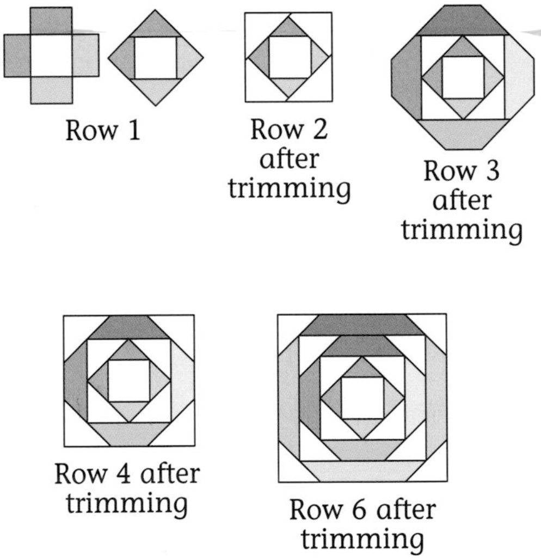

Row 1 Row 2 after trimming Row 3 after trimming

Row 4 after trimming Row 6 after trimming

2. ASSEMBLE: Stitch blocks together into horizontal rows, rotated as shown. Stitch rows together. Press well.

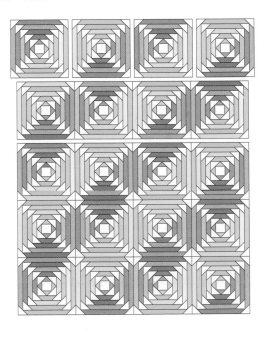

Continued on page 46.

47 x 47″ • 9″ Block

Water Lilies features four different blocks arranged symmetrically for a unique look.

Yardage
Choose fabrics with 42″ usable width.

Blocks	⅞ yd dark olive
	¾ yd fuchsia
	½ yd each dark blue, light blue, green
	¼ yd each light green, olive
Border 1	⅓ yd
Border 2	¾ yd purple/olive/blue print
Binding	½ yd
Backing	3 yd
Batting	51 x 51″

Cutting
Cut strips from selvage to selvage.

Blocks	dark olive	16 squares 3½″
	dark olive	9 strips 2″ wide
	fuchsia	11 strips 2″ wide
	dark blue	6 strips 2″ wide
	light blue	7 strips 2″ wide
	green	7 strips 2″ wide
	lt green	3 strips 2″ wide
	olive	2 strips 2″ wide
Border 1		4 strips 2″ wide
Border 2		5 strips 4½″ wide
Binding		5 strips 2½″ wide

Directions
Sew ¼″ seams unless otherwise noted.

1. CORNER BLOCK:

Cut 2″ strips into segments. Cut only the number of segments in the third column, saving the rest of the strip(s) for center and side blocks.

Row 1	3½″ segments	16	dark blue
Row 2	5½″ segments	16	light blue
Row 3	5½″ segments	8	green
		8	light green
Row 4	7″ segments	12	dark olive
		4	fuchsia
Row 5	4″ segments	12	fuchsia
		4	olive

Make 4 blocks. See Pineapple Rule® Directions, pages 3-6. Corner finish is similar to Corner B on page 6. Use diagrams starting on this page for color placement.

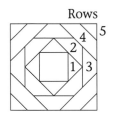

Rows	COLORS
	Dark olive = DO
	Olive = O
	Green = G
	Light green = LG
	Dark blue = DB
	Light blue = LB
	Fuchsia = F

Corner Block
Make 4

CENTER BLOCK:

Cut 2″ strips into segments:

Row 1	3½″ segments	16	dark blue
Row 2	5½″ segments	16	fuchsia
Row 3	5½″ segments	16	green
Row 4	7″ segments	8	dark olive
		8	fuchsia
Row 5	4″ segments	8	fuchsia
		8	olive

Make 4 blocks. See Pineapple Rule® Directions, pages 3-6.

Center Block
Make 4

Continued on page 45.

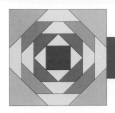

Twilight

52 x 62" • 8" Block Corner A

The blocks for this quilt are identical, made with blue and purple diagonal rows. The teal sashing stars add interest.

Yardage
Choose fabrics with 42" usable width.

Block	¼ yd dark purple - centers
	¼ yd each of dark blue, medium dark purple - Row 2
	⅓ yd each of medium dark blue, medium purple - Row 4
	¾ yd each of medium blue, light purple - Row 6
Block, sashing	2½ yd pink
Stars	⅞ yd dark teal
	⅓ yd light teal
Border	¾ yd purple/teal
Binding	½ yd
Backing	3½ yd
Batting	58 x 68"

Cutting
Cut strips from selvage to selvage.

Block	dk purple	20 squares 2½" - centers
	dk blue	4 strips 1½" wide - Row 2
	med dk purple	4 strips 1½" wide - Row 2
	med dk blue	5 strips 1½" wide - Row 4
	med purple	5 strips 1½" wide - Row 4
	med blue	7 strips 3¼" wide - Row 6
	lt purple	7 strips 3¼" wide - Row 6
	pink	23 strips 1½" wide - Rows 1, 3, 5
Sashing	pink	20 squares 1½"
		18 pieces 1½ x 8½"
		38 pieces 1½ x 2½"
		49 pieces 2½ x 8½"
Stars	dk teal	408 squares 1½"
	lt teal	34 squares 2½"
Border		5 strips 4½" wide
Binding		6 strips 2¼" wide

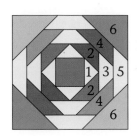

Rows

Directions
Sew ¼" seams unless otherwise noted.

1. BLOCKS:
   Cut 1½" blue & purple strips into segments:

Row 2	3½" segments	40 pieces each
Row 4	5" segments	40 pieces each

   Cut 3¼" blue & purple strips into segments:

   | Row 6 | 6" segments | 40 pieces each |

   Cut 1½" pink strips into segments:

Row 1	2½" segments	80 pieces
Row 3	4" segments	80 pieces
Row 5	5" segments	80 pieces

   Make 20 blocks. See Pineapple Rule® Directions, pages 3-6.

2. SASHING: Using diagrams, make 38 small star point units, 34 square-in-a-square units, and 49 large star point units. Press.

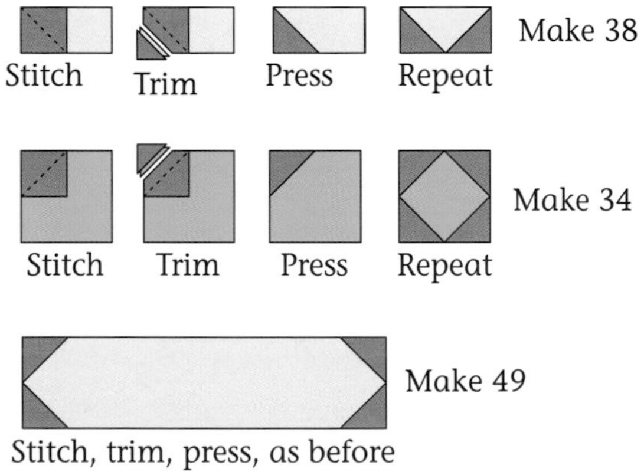

Stitch   Trim   Press   Repeat   Make 38

Stitch   Trim   Press   Repeat   Make 34

Make 49

Stitch, trim, press, as before

Make 2 top/bottom sashing rows, adding 1½" squares to each end, as shown on page 46. Press. Make 6 sashing rows as shown. Press. Make 5 sashing/block rows, adding 1½ x 8½" pieces to each end, as shown. Press. Save remaining units for Step 4.

Continued on page 46.

Island Tango

60x76" • 16" Block Corner B

In Island Tango, each block is different, and there are no organized light and dark areas. Centers and strips for rows are cut twice as wide of those for an 8" block.

Yardage
Choose fabrics with 42" usable width.

Block	1¼ yd blue floral print - center & Row 7
	⅜ yd each of 18 red, pink, orange, tan & green floral prints - Rows 1-6
Border 1	⅓ yd
Border 2	1⅓ yd
Binding	⅝ yd
Backing	4 yd
Batting	66x82"

Cutting
Cut strips from selvage to selvage.

Blocks	blue	12 squares 4½" - centers
		8 strips 3¼" wide - Row 7
	others	64 strips 2½" wide - Rows 1-6
Border 1		6 strips 1½" wide
Border 2		7 strips 5½" wide
Binding		7 strips 2½" wide

Directions
Sew ¼" seams unless otherwise noted.

1. BLOCKS:
   Stack 2½" floral strips and cut into segments. Cut segments of different lengths from each stack to distribute fabrics among rows.

Row 1	4½" segments	48 pieces
Row 2	6¼" segments	48 pieces
Row 3	7" segments	48 pieces
Row 4	8½" segments	48 pieces
Row 5	8½" segments	48 pieces
Row 6	10½" segments	48 pieces

   Stack 3¼" blue floral strips and cut into segments:

Row 7	6½" segments	48 pieces

   Make 12 blocks. See Pineapple Rule® Directions, pages 3-6. Placement of lights and darks is not planned. Pick up segments at random to make each block different.

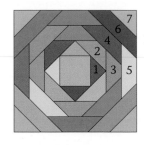

Rows

2. ASSEMBLE: Stitch blocks together into horizontal rows. Stitch rows together. Press.

3. BORDER 1: Stitch strips end to end. Press. Cut strips to fit sides of quilt. Stitch to quilt. Press. Repeat at top and bottom. Diagram on page 47.

Continued on page 47.

23

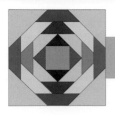

Provence

56 x 67" • 8" Block Corner A

Two blocks make this quilt, each with different centers and yellows. The blues and teals repeat in both blocks.

Yardage
Choose fabrics with 42" usable width.

Block	
	⅛ yd each of 2 oranges - centers
	¼ yd each teal & dark blue - Row 1
	¼ yd each teal & medium blue - Row 3
	⅓ yd each teal & medium blue - Row 5
	¼ yd each of 2 yellows - Row 2
	⅓ yd each of 2 yellows - Row 4
	⅔ yd each of 2 yellows - Row 6

Center panel,
   border triangles   2¼ yd yellow
   more may be needed if motif on center panel must be centered

Border triangles	1⅛ yd dark blue
Binding	⅝ yd
Backing	3¾ yd
Batting	62 x 73"

Cutting
Cut strips from selvage to selvage.

*Cut these squares in **half** diagonally.
Cut these squares in **quarters diagonally.

Block	oranges	9 squares 2½" of each - centers
	teal	3 strips 1½" wide - Row 1
	dk blue	3 strips 1½" wide - Row 1
	teal	4 strips 1½" wide - Row 3
	med blue	4 strips 1½" wide - Row 3
	teal	5 strips 1½" wide - Row 5
	med blue	5 strips 1½" wide - Row 5
	yellows	4 strips each 1½" wide - Row 2
		5 strips each 1½" wide - Row 4
		6 strips each 3¼" wide - Row 6
Center panel	yellow	34½ x 45¾"
Border triangles	yellow	**4 squares 12⅝"
		*2 squares 6⅝"
Border triangles	dk blue	**4 squares 12⅝"
	dk blue	*6 squares 6⅝"
Binding		7 strips 2¼" wide

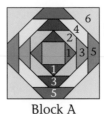

Block A   Block B

Directions
Sew ¼" seams unless otherwise noted.

1. BLOCKS:

   Cut 1½" teal & blue strips into segments:

Row 1	2½" segments	36 pieces each
Row 3	4" segments	36 pieces each
Row 5	5" segments	36 pieces each

   Cut 1½" yellow strips into segments:

Row 2	3½" segments	36 pieces each
Row 4	5" segments	36 pieces each

   Cut 3¼" yellow strips into segments:

Row 6	6" segments	36 pieces each

   Make 9 Block A and 9 Block B. Use one center orange in Block A and other in Block B. Use one Row 2 (Row 4, Row 6) yellow in Block A and the other in Block B. Note placement of teals and blues. See Pineapple Rule® Directions, pages 3-6.

2. BORDER: Make borders as shown. Stitch side borders to center panel. Press. Stitch top and bottom borders to center panel. Additional diagram on page 47.

Left Side - Blocks B-A-B-A - Make 1

Right Side - Blocks B-A-B-A - Make 1

Top - Blocks A-B-A-B-A - Make 1

Bottom - Blocks B-A-B-A B - Make 1

24

Continued on page 47.

Barn Dance

68 x 92" • 12" Block Corner A

Barn Dance is made with scrappy blocks—lights for the side rows and darks for the diagonal rows.

Yardage   Choose fabrics with 42" usable width.

Blocks	lights	¼ yd each of 20 fabrics
	darks	¼ yd each of 35 fabrics
Border 1		½ yd
Border 2		⅛ yd each of 12 or more fabrics
Binding		¾ yd
Backing		5⅞ yd
Batting		74 x 98"

Cutting   Cut strips from selvage to selvage.

Block	lights	5 strips 1½" wide from each fabric Rows 1, 3, 5, 7, 9
	darks	1 strip 4¼" wide from each of 28 fabrics - Row 10 1 square 2½" from each of 35 fabrics - centers strips 1½" wide from remaining fabric - Rows 2, 4, 6, 8
Border 1		8 strips 1½" wide
Border 2		56 pieces 3½ x 6½"
Binding		9 strips 2½" wide

Directions   Sew ¼" seams unless otherwise noted.

1. BLOCKS:

    Stack 1½" light strips and cut into segments. Cut segments of different lengths from each stack to distribute fabrics among rows.

Row 1	2½" segments	140 pieces
Row 3	4" segments	140 pieces
Row 5	5" segments	140 pieces
Row 7	6" segments	140 pieces
Row 9	6½" segments	140 pieces

    Stack 1½" dark strips and cut into segments.

Row 2	3½" segments	140 pieces
Row 4	5" segments	140 pieces
Row 6	6" segments	140 pieces
Row 8	6½" segments	140 pieces

    Stack 4¼" dark strips and cut into segments.

Row 10	7½" segments	140 pieces

    Make 35 blocks. See Pineapple Rule® Directions, pages 3-6.

2. ASSEMBLE: Stitch blocks together into horizontal rows. Stitch rows together. Press well.

3. BORDER 1: Stitch strips together end to end using straight, not diagonal, seams. Press. Cut 2 pieces to fit sides of quilt. Stitch to quilt. Press. Repeat at top and bottom.

4. BORDER 2: Stitch 16 of the 3½ x 6½" pieces together end to end for each side border. Stitch 12 pieces together end to end for top and bottom borders. Press. Trim an equal amount off each end of each side border to make the borders symmetrical and to make them the same length as the quilt. Stitch side borders to quilt. Press. Repeat at top and bottom. Diagrams on page 48.

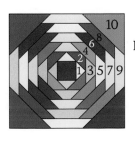

Rows

Continued on page 48.

Mocha Latte

60 x 72″ • 12″ Block Corner B

Blocks in Mocha Latte have scrappy diagonal rows of blacks in one direction and browns in the other.

Yardage   Choose fabrics with 42″ usable width.

Blocks	blacks	½ yd each of 9 fabrics
	browns	½ yd each of 9 fabrics
	creams	⅓ yd each of 12 fabrics
Border 1		⅜ yd
Border 2		1⅓ yd
Binding		⅝ yd
Backing		4 yd
Batting		66 x 78″

Cutting   Cut strips from selvage to selvage.

Block	blacks	5 strips 1½″ wide from each fabric
		Rows 2, 4, 6, 8, 10, 11
		1 strip 2¼″ wide from each fabric
		Row 12
		20 squares 2½″ - centers
	browns	5 strips 1½″ wide from each fabric
		Rows 1, 2, 4, 6, 8, 10, 11
		1 strip 2¼″ wide from each fabric
		Row 12
	creams	4 strips 1½″ wide from each fabric
		Rows 3, 5, 7, 9
Border 1		6 strips 1½″ wide
Border 2		7 strips 5½″ wide
Binding		7 strips 2½″ wide

Directions   Sew ¼″ seams unless otherwise noted.

1. BLOCKS:

   Stack 1½″ black strips and cut into segments. Cut segments of different lengths from each stack to distribute fabrics among rows.

Row 2	3½″ segments	40 pieces
Row 4	5″ segments	40 pieces
Row 6	6″ segments	40 pieces
Row 8	6½″ segments	40 pieces
Row 10	7½″ segments	40 pieces
Row 11	5½″ segments	40 pieces

   Stack 2¼″ black strips and cut into segments.

   | Row 12 | 3½″ segments | 40 pieces |

   Stack 1½″ brown strips and cut into segments.

Row 1	2½″ segments	80 pieces
Row 2	3½″ segments	40 pieces
Row 4	5″ segments	40 pieces
Row 6	6″ segments	40 pieces
Row 8	6½″ segments	40 pieces
Row 10	7½″ segments	40 pieces
Row 11	5½″ segments	40 pieces

   Stack 2¼″ brown strips and cut into segments.

   | Row 12 | 3½″ segments | 40 pieces |

   Stack 1½″ cream strips and cut into segments.

Row 3	4″ segments	80 pieces
Row 5	5″ segments	80 pieces
Row 7	6″ segments	80 pieces
Row 9	6½″ segments	80 pieces

   Make 20 blocks. See Pineapple Rule® Directions, pages 3-6. Note Row 12 color reversal.

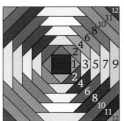

Rows

2. ASSEMBLE: Stitch blocks together into horizontal rows, oriented as shown. Stitch rows together. Press.

Continued on page 48.

63 x 63" • 15" Block

In Peppermint Garden, four-patches form the centers, greens and reds create the diagonal rows, and seamed pieces complete the corners.

Yardage
Choose fabrics with 42" usable width.

Blocks, applique	⅞ yd red #1 - darkest
	⅜ yd red #2
	½ yd red #3
	⅝ yd red #4
	1⅛ yd green #1 - darkest
	½ yd each - greens #2, #3, #4
Blocks, Border 3	3⅜ yd cream
Border 1	⅜ yd
Border 2	⅝ yd
Binding	⅝ yd
Backing	4⅛ yd
Batting	69 x 69"

Cutting
Cut strips from selvage to selvage.

Blocks	red #1	6 strips 2" wide
		2 strips 3½" - corners
	red #2	3 strips 2" wide
	red #3	4 strips 2" wide
	red #4	4 strips 2" wide
	green #1	6 strips 2" wide
		2 strips 3½" - corners
	green #2	3 strips 2" wide
	green #3	4 strips 2" wide
	green #4	4 strips 2" wide
	cream	26 strips 2" wide - blocks
		4 strips 3½" - corners
Applique		See Step 4 on page 49 - cut vines 1st - see patterns on page 54
Border 1		7 strips 1½" wide
Border 2		7 strips 2½" wide
Border 3	cream	7 strips 6½" wide
Binding		7 strips 2½" wide

Directions
Sew ¼" seams unless otherwise noted.

1. BLOCKS:

Cut 2" cream strips into segments:

Row 1	3½" segments	36 pieces
Row 3	5½" segments	36 pieces
Row 5	7" segments	36 pieces
Row 7	8" segments	36 pieces

Cut 3½" cream strips into segments:

| Row 9 | 3½" segments | 36 pieces |

Set aside one 2" red #1 strip for block centers.

Cut 2" red #1 strips into segments:

| Row 8 | 9½" segments | 18 pieces |

Cut 3½" red #1 strips into segments:

| Row 9 | 3½" segments | 18 pieces |

Cut 2" red #2 strips into segments:

| Row 2 | 5" segments | 18 pieces |

Cut 2" red #3 strips into segments:

| Row 4 | 7" segments | 18 pieces |

Cut 2" red #4 strips into segments:

| Row 6 | 8" segments | 18 pieces |

Set aside one 2" green #1 strip for block centers.

Cut 2" green #1 strips into segments:

| Row 8 | 9½" segments | 18 pieces |

Cut 3½" green #1 strips into segments:

| Row 9 | 3½" segments | 18 pieces |

Cut 2" green #2 strips into segments:

| Row 2 | 5" segments | 18 pieces |

Cut 2" green #3 strips into segments:

| Row 4 | 7" segments | 18 pieces |

Cut 2" green #4 strips into segments:

| Row 6 | 8" segments | 18 pieces |

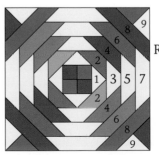

Rows

Continued on page 49.

First Place Traditional winner in the 2425 P&B Textiles Morning Garden Quilt
Challenge using fabric designed by Alex Anderson. Made by Nancy Smith.

62 x 73″ • 8″ Block Corner A

Poppies has two blocks with specific placement of red and purple fabrics. A single black is used for the centers and diagonal rows.

Yardage — Choose fabrics with 42″ usable width.

Block A	⅙ yd red/purple - Row 1
	¼ yd each of 2 reds - Rows 3, 5
Block B	⅙ yd light purple - Row 1
	¼ yd each of 2 reds - Rows 3, 5
Blocks, sashing, Borders 2, 3, 4	3¾ yd black
Setting triangles	½ yd each of 2 reds - left panel
	½ yd each of 2 reds - right panel
	½ yd each of 2 purples - panels
Applique, Border 1	¼ yd each of 6 oranges - flowers
Applique	⅛ yd dark red - flower centers
	⅜ yd green - vines, leaves
	⅙ yd each of 2 greens - leaves, buds
Border 3	⅝ yd purple
Binding	⅔ yd
Backing	4⅝ yd
Batting	68 x 79″

Cutting — Cut strips from selvage to selvage.

*Cut these squares in **half** diagonally.
Cut these squares in **quarters diagonally.

Block A	red/purple	2 strips 1½″ wide - Row 1
	red	4 strips 1½″ wide - Row 3
	red	4 strips 1½″ wide - Row 5
Block B	lt purple	2 strips 1½″ wide - Row 1
	red	4 strips 1½″ wide - Row 3
	red	4 strips 1½″ wide - Row 5
Black		3 strips 6¼″ wide - vertical sashing
		15 squares 2½″ - block centers
		14 strips 1½″ wide - Rows 2, 4
		10 strips 3¼″ wide - Row 6
		6 strips 2½″ wide - Border 2
		*24 squares 2⅞″ - Border 3 triangles
		7 strips 4½″ wide - Border 4

Setting triangles	left panel - from each of 2 reds	
	*1 square 6⅝″	
	**1 square 12⅝″	
	right panel - from each of 2 reds	
	*1 square 6⅝″	
	**1 square 12⅝″	
	panels - from each of 2 purples	
	*2 squares 6⅝″	
	**2 squares 12⅝″	
Applique	See Step 3 on page 50 - cut vines 1st - see patterns on page 55	
Border 1	25 pieces 1 x 9-12″	
Border 3 - purple	*24 squares 2⅞″	
	4 squares 2½″	
	4 strips 2½″ wide	
Binding	7-8 strips 2½″ wide	

Directions — Sew ¼″ seams unless otherwise noted.

1. BLOCK A:

Cut 1½″ red strips into segments:

Row 1	2½″ segments	32 pieces
Row 3	4″ segments	32 pieces
Row 5	5″ segments	32 pieces

Cut 1½″ black strips into segments:

Row 2	3½″ segments	32 pieces
Row 4	5″ segments	32 pieces

Cut 3¼″ black strips into segments:

Row 6	6″ segments	32 pieces

Make 8 blocks. See Pineapple Rule® Directions, pages 3-6.

BLOCK B:

Repeat the above, substituting light purple and reds cut for Rows 1, 3, and 5 of Block B. Cut 28 pieces for each row. Make 7 blocks.

Rows   Rows

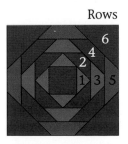 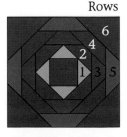

Block A - Make 8   Block B - Make 7

Continued on page 50.

Pillow pattern on page 37.

Pineapple Pizzazz

72 x 88″ • 13½″ Block Corner B

Directions for Pineapple Pizzazz include diagrams specific to the block, so use of Pineapple Rule® Directions at front of book is not required. The diagonal rows in each block are scrappy, and the same red is used for the side rows.

Yardage Choose fabric with 42″ usable width.

Blocks
Centers	¼ yd black	
Rows	¼ yd each of 25 brights	
	3¼ yd red	
Border 1	⅞ yd red	
Border 2	½ yd black & white check	
Border 3	1 yd black	
	1⅛ yd white	
Border 4	1 yd black	
Binding	¾ yd	
Backing	5⅝ yd	
Batting	78 x 94″	

Cutting Cut strips from selvage to selvage.

*Cut these squares in half diagonally.

Blocks	black	20 squares 2¼″ - centers
	brights	80-85 strips 1¾″ wide
	red	60 strips 1¾″ wide
Border 1		4 strips 2½″ wide - sides
		4 strips 3¾″ wide - top/bottom
Border 2		7 strips 1½″ wide
Border 3		*68 squares 2⅞″ - black
		*68 squares 2⅞″ - white
		*136 squares 1⅞″ - black
		*136 squares 1⅞″ - white
		4 squares 3½″ - white
Border 4		8 strips 3½″ wide
Binding		9 strips 2½″ wide

Directions Sew ¼″ seams unless otherwise noted.

1. Stack 1¾″ strips and cut into segments. Cut segments of different lengths from each stack to distribute fabrics among rows.

Brights
Row 2	3″ segments	80 pieces
Row 4	5″ segments	80 pieces
Row 6	6″ segments	80 pieces
Row 8	7″ segments	80 pieces
Row 10	8″ segments	80 pieces
Row 11	5½″ segments	80 pieces
Row 12	3″ segments	80 pieces

Red
Row 1	2¼″ segments	80 pieces
Row 3	4″ segments	80 pieces
Row 5	6″ segments	80 pieces
Row 7	7″ segments	80 pieces
Row 9	8″ segments	80 pieces

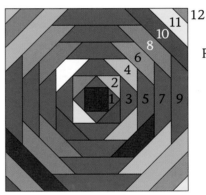

Rows

2. Make 20 blocks as follows:

Row 1: Mark diagonal lines from corner to corner across wrong side of center square. Stitch Row 1 pieces to opposite sides of center square. Repeat on remaining sides. Carefully press seam allowances toward outside of block; do not stretch square out of shape.

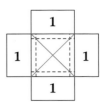

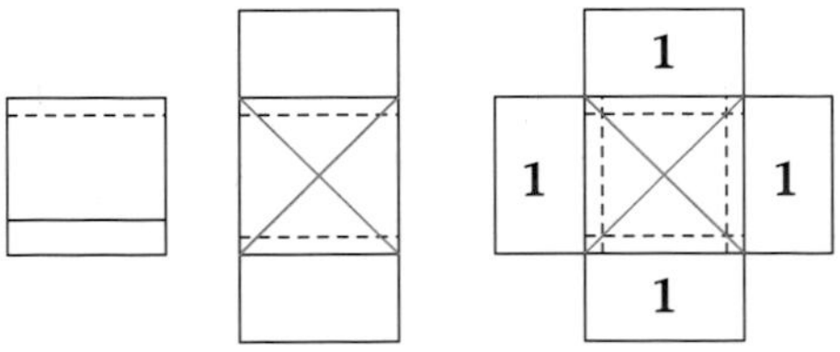

34

Continued on page 51.

Place Mats

14 x 18″   Photo on page 11.

Yardage
Choose fabrics with 42″ usable width.

For 2 place mats:

Dark - centers	⅙ yd
Darks	⅛ yd each of 7 fabrics
Lights	⅛ yd each of 6 fabrics
Binding	⅜ yd
Backing	⅝ yd
Batting - firm cotton	2 pieces 20 x 20″

Cutting
Cut strips from selvage to selvage.

Dark - centers	2 squares 3½″
Darks	1 strip 2½″ wide of each fabric
Lights	1 strip 2½″ wide of each fabric
Binding	4 strips 2½″ wide
Backing	2 pieces 20 x 20″

Directions
Sew ¼″ seams unless otherwise noted.

1. Cut 2½″ strips into segments.

Row 1	3½″ segments	8 pieces
Row 2	5″ segments	8 pieces
Row 3	7″ segments	8 pieces
Row 4	7″ segments	8 pieces
Row 5	8½″ segments	8 pieces
Row 6	8½″ segments	8 pieces
Row 7	10½″ segments	4 pieces

2. Place batting on wrong side of backing. Draw lines on batting from corner to corner. Pin center square, right side up, to batting where diagonal lines cross, matching corners of square to diagonal lines.

3. Place Row 1 piece right side down on top edge of center square, raw edges even. Stitch through all layers. Flip Row 1 piece over and press. Repeat on remaining 3 edges of center square.

4. Place Pineapple Rule® on place mat, **inside diagonal lines on ruler on top of seam lines and center vertical line matching marked line on batting**. Mark a cutting line across Row 1 pieces. Using scissors, cut on drawn line **through fabric only**. You may have to snip a few stitches where sewing lines intersect. Repeat on all sides. Repeat for Rows 2 and 3.

5. Beginning with Row 4, line up edge of ruler with edge of previous row rather than using inside diagonal lines. Row 7 goes on sides only. Press well. Trim batting and backing even with fabric.

6. Stitch binding strips end to end. Press in half lengthwise, wrong sides together. Bind place mats using ⅜″ seam allowance.

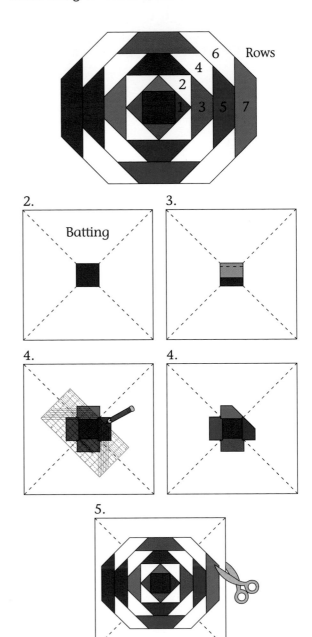

36

Pin Cushion

6″ Square   Photo on page 38.

Yardage   Choose fabrics with 42″ usable width.

Darks   scraps for paper piecing
Lights   scraps for paper piecing
Backing   ¼ yd
Fiberfill   small amount

Directions

1. Paper piece one 6″ block. See directions and diagrams on page 38, pattern and cutting chart on page 39.

2. Cut backing 8x8″. Center and pin block to backing, right sides together. Stitch around block, leaving an opening on one side for turning. Trim backing even with block. Clip corners, turn, and press. Stuff firmly with fiberfill. Stitch opening closed.

Key Chain or Pin

2½″ Square   Photo on page 38.

Choose fabric scraps for paper piecing and border/backing. Choose very thin cotton batting or flannel scrap for filler.

Paper piece one 2″ block with border. See directions and diagrams on page 38, pattern on page 39.

Cut 3½″ squares of backing and filler. Place backing wrong side down on filler. Center block right sides together on backing. Stitch around block, leaving an opening on one side for turning. Trim backing and filler to same size as block. Clip corners and turn right side out. Press. Stitch opening closed. Quilt as desired.

For key chain, apply ½″ eyelet to one corner and attach 1¼″ key ring to eyelet. For pin, stitch or hot glue pinback to back of block.

Pillow

16″ Square   Photo on page 32.

Yardage   Choose fabrics with 42″ usable width.

Darks & lights   scraps for paper piecing
Border, envelope back   ¾ yd
Backing & batting for quilting   20x20″
Binding   ¼ yd
Pillow form   16″

Directions   Sew ¼″ seams unless otherwise noted.

1. PILLOW TOP: Paper piece four 6″ blocks. See directions and diagrams on page 38, pattern and cutting chart on page 39. Stitch blocks together in two rows of two. Press. Cut 2 envelope back pieces 20x16½″. Set aside. Cut 2 border pieces 2½x12½″ and 2 border pieces 2½x16½″. Stitch short border pieces to opposite sides of block. Press. Repeat with long pieces on remaining sides. Layer backing, batting, and pillow top. Quilt as desired. Trim backing and batting to same size as pillow top.

2. ENVELOPE BACK: Press envelope back pieces in half, to 10x16½″. Place backing pieces on wrong side of quilted pillow top, raw edges matching, folded edges overlapping at center of pillow. Stitch around outside edge a scant ½″ from edge. Test fit by trying pillow cover on pillow form—adjust fit if necessary—trim seam allowance to ½″ if adjustment made seam allowance larger.

3. BINDING: Cut 2 strips 3¼″ wide by width of fabric. Stitch strips together end to end. Press in half lengthwise, wrong sides together. Bind pillow using ½″ seam allowance.

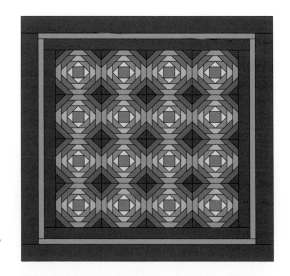

Try making a wall hanging with 6″ paper-pieced blocks. This example is 33″ square and has 1½″, ¾″, and 2¼″ borders. Paper-piecing pattern, page 39.

Paper Piecing

Cut out pattern, leaving a margin outside dotted cutting line.

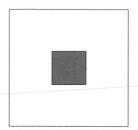

Place center square, right side up, on wrong side of pattern, overlapping center square on pattern by ¼" on each side.

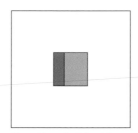

Place Piece 2, right side down, on center square.

Flip pattern over, top to bottom, and stitch on line, adding a few stitches at either end. Use short stitch length.

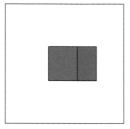

Press Piece 2 to right side.

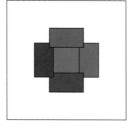

Repeat stitching and pressing with Pieces 3-5.

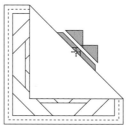

Fold paper on line, pulling it away from ends of stitching lines so it crosses corner of center square. Trim, leaving ¼" seam allowance. Repeat on other corners.

Repeat stitching, pressing, and trimming with Pieces 6-9.

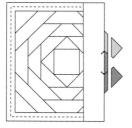

Repeat stitching and pressing with Pieces 10-17. Trim after each round, folding paper on line and pulling it away from ends of stitching lines.

Repeat stitching, pressing, and trimming with pieces 18-21.

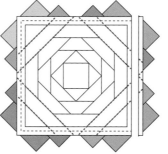

Repeat stitching and pressing with pieces 22-29—stitch to edge of paper at each end of each piece. Trim block on dotted line.

Paper can be removed now or after blocks are sewn together.

Pincushion
Keychain
Pin

Paper Piecing

CUTTING FOR 6″ BLOCK

Cut strips the width of the first measurement, then cut strips into segments using the second measurement.

Piece 1	2 x 2″
Pieces 2-5	1⅜ x 2″
Pieces 6-9	1⅜ x 2⅝″
Pieces 10-13	1⅜ x 3″
Pieces 14-17	1⅜ x 3½″
Pieces 18-21	1⅜ x 3½″
Pieces 22-25	1⅜ x 4½″
Pieces 26-29	1¾ x 3″

2″ Block with Border

Key Chain & Pin

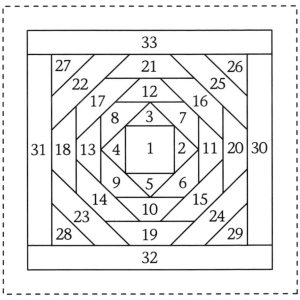

6″ Block

Pillow, Pincushion, & Wall Hanging

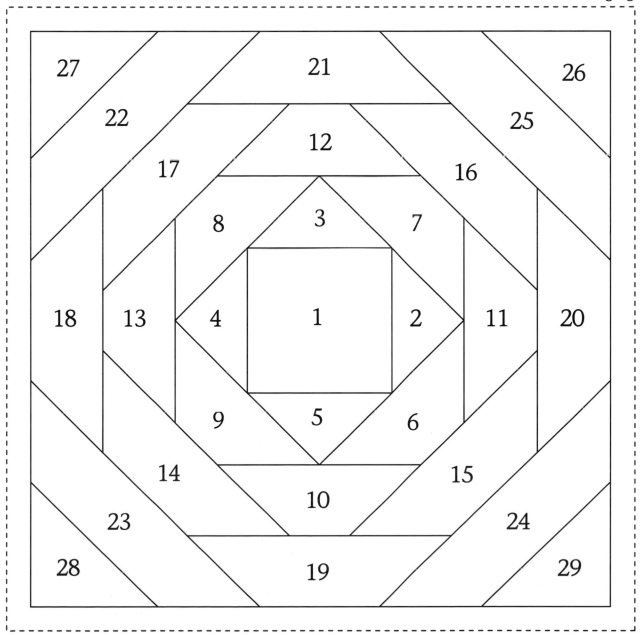

39

Ann Petersen
Pineapple Snowflake
30 x 30″

Ann Petersen
Prickly Pineapple
33 x 33″

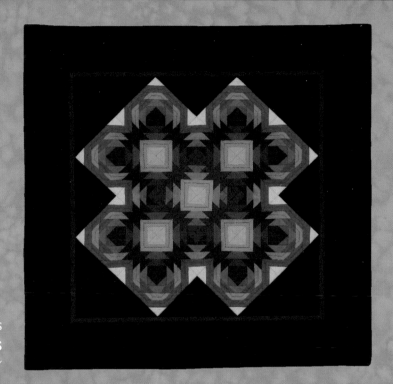

Sharon Holmes
Amish Blossoms
23x23″

Shellie Hunter
**Black & White &
Red All Over**
50x61″

41

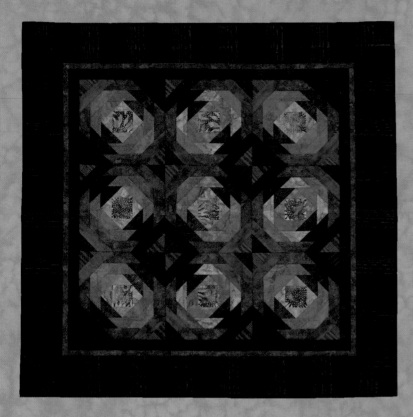

Susan Johnson
Tlaquepaque Pineapple
34 x 34″

Possibilities®
Spice Rack
44 x 55″

Possibilities®
Sunrise
33 x 33″

Barbara Karst
**Snake in the
Pineapple Patch**
45 x 45″

Which Witch?

Continued from page 12.

4. BORDER 1: Stitch strips end to end using straight, not diagonal, seams. Press. Cut 2 pieces to fit sides of quilt. Stitch to quilt. Press. Repeat at top and bottom.

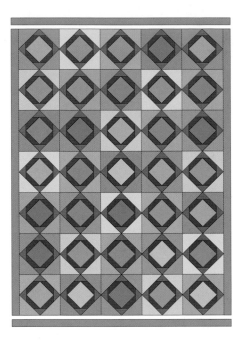

5. BORDERS 2 & 3: Repeat Step 4.

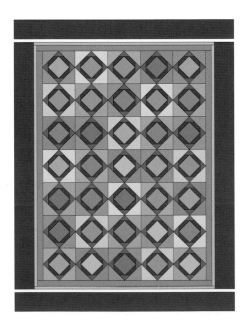

6. LAYER & QUILT: Piece backing horizontally to same size as batting. Layer and quilt as desired. Trim backing and batting even with quilt top.

7. BIND: Stitch binding strips end to end. Press in half lengthwise, wrong sides together. Bind quilt using 3/8" seam allowance.

Bundle of Joy

Continued from page 14.

4. LAYER & QUILT: Cut backing to same size as batting. Layer and quilt as desired. Trim backing and batting even with quilt top.

5. BIND: Stitch binding strips end to end. Press in half lengthwise, wrong sides together. Bind quilt using 3/8" seam allowance.

Bundle of Joy Blue Version

Yardage Choose fabrics with 42" usable width.

Block 1/4 yd medium blue - centers
1/2 yd medium light blue - Row 2
5/8 yd medium light blue - Row 4
3/4 yd light blue - Row 6
1/3 yd each of 2 light yellows - Row 7
1/3 yd medium light green - Row 1
1/2 yd medium light green - Row 3
5/8 yd medium light green - Row 5

Follow yardage chart on page 14 for remaining fabrics.

Cutting Cut strips from selvage to selvage.

Follow cutting chart on page 14, using row designations and changing color names.

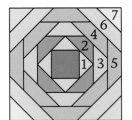

Rows

Directions Sew 1/4" seams unless otherwise noted.

Follow directions on page 14, using row designations and changing color names.

Water Lilies

Continued from page 18.

SIDE BLOCK A:

Cut 2″ strips into segments:

Row 1	3½″ segments	16	dark blue
Row 2	5½″ segments	16	light blue
Row 3	5½″ segments	12	green
		4	light green
Row 4	7″ segments	12	dark olive
		4	fuchsia
Row 5	4″ segments	12	fuchsia
		4	olive

Make 4 blocks. See Pineapple Rule® Directions, pages 3-6.

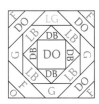 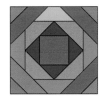

Side Block A
Make 4

SIDE BLOCK B: Use chart above. Block B is mirror image of Block A. Make 4 blocks.

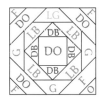 

Side Block B
Make 4

2. ASSEMBLE: Arrange blocks as shown, rotating as needed. Stitch into horizontal rows. Stitch rows together. Press.

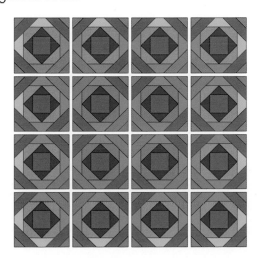

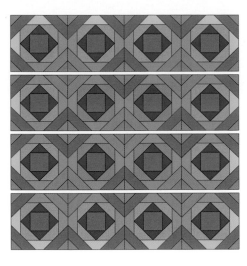

3. BORDER 1: Cut 2 strips to fit sides of quilt. Stitch to quilt. Press. Repeat at top and bottom.

4. BORDER 2: Cut 2 strips to fit sides of quilt. Stitch to quilt. Press. Stitch remaining 3 strips end to end using straight, not diagonal, seams. Press. Cut 2 pieces to fit top and bottom of quilt. Stitch to quilt. Press.

5. LAYER & QUILT: Piece backing to same size as batting. Layer and quilt as desired. Trim backing and batting even with quilt top.

6. BIND: Stitch binding strips end to end. Press in half lengthwise, wrong sides together. Bind quilt using ⅜″ seam allowance.

Strawberries & Cream

Continued from page 10.

5. BORDERS 2 & 3: Repeat Step 4.

6. LAYER & QUILT: Cut backing to same size as batting. Layer and quilt as desired. Trim backing and batting even with quilt top.

7. BIND: Stitch binding strips end to end. Press in half lengthwise, wrong sides together. Bind quilt using ⅜″ seam allowance.

Jellybeans

Continued from page 16.

3. BORDER 1: Stitch strips together end to end using straight, not diagonal, seams. Press. Cut 2 pieces to fit sides of quilt. Stitch to quilt. Press. Repeat at top and bottom.

4. BORDERS 2 & 3: Repeat Step 3.

5. LAYER & QUILT: Piece backing horizontally to same size as batting. Layer and quilt as desired. Trim backing and batting even with quilt top.

6. BIND: Stitch binding strips end to end. Press in half lengthwise, wrong sides together. Bind quilt using ⅜″ seam allowance.

Twilight

Continued from page 20.

Top/Bottom - Make 2

Sashing Row - Make 6

Sashing/Block Row - Make 5

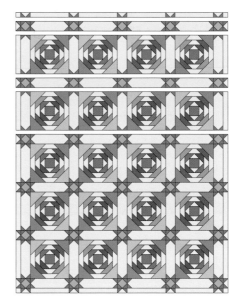

3. ASSEMBLE: Stitch rows made in Step 2 together. Press.

4. BORDER: Make 4 corner blocks as shown. Press.

  Make 4

Stitch border strips end to end using straight, not diagonal, seams. Press. Cut 2 pieces the same width as quilt and 2 pieces the same length as quilt. Stitch side pieces to quilt. Press. Stitch corner blocks to each end of top and bottom border pieces. Stitch to quilt. Press.

5. LAYER & QUILT: Piece backing horizontally to same size as batting. Layer and quilt as desired. Trim backing and batting even with quilt top.

6. BIND: Stitch binding strips end to end. Press in half lengthwise, wrong sides together. Bind quilt using ¼″ seam allowance.

Island Tango

Continued from page 22.

4. BORDER 2: Repeat Step 3.

5. LAYER & QUILT: Piece backing horizontally to same size as batting. Layer and quilt as desired. Trim backing and batting even with quilt top.

6. BIND: Stitch binding strips end to end. Press in half lengthwise, wrong sides together. Bind quilt using ⅜″ seam allowance.

Provence

Continued from page 24.

3. LAYER & QUILT: Piece backing horizontally to same size as batting. Layer and quilt as desired. Trim backing and batting even with quilt top.

4. BIND: Stitch binding strips end to end. Press in half lengthwise, wrong sides together. Bind quilt using ¼″ seam allowance.

Barn Dance

Continued from page 26.

Sides - 16 pieces - Make 2

Top & bottom - 12 pieces - Make 2

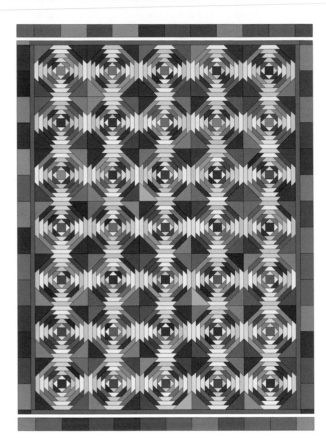

5. LAYER & QUILT: Piece backing vertically to same size as batting. Layer and quilt as desired. Trim backing and batting even with quilt top.

6. BIND: Stitch binding strips end to end. Press in half lengthwise, wrong sides together. Bind quilt using ⅜″ seam allowance.

Mocha Latte

Continued from page 28.

3. BORDER 1: Stitch strips together end to end using straight, not diagonal, seams. Press. Cut 2 pieces to fit sides of quilt. Stitch to quilt. Press. Repeat at top and bottom.

4. BORDER 2: Repeat Step 3.

5. LAYER & QUILT: Piece backing horizontally to same size as batting. Layer and quilt as desired. Trim backing and batting even with quilt top.

6. BIND: Stitch binding strips end to end. Press in half lengthwise, wrong sides together. Bind quilt using ⅜″ seam allowance.

Peppermint Garden

Continued from page 30.

BLOCK CENTERS: Stitch reserved red #1 and green #1 strips into a strip set. Press. Cut into 2″ segments. Stitch segments together as shown to make 9 four-patch units. Press. Use these for center square when constructing block.

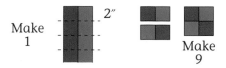

Make 1

Make 9

BLOCK ROWS 1-8: Make 9 blocks, stopping after Row 8. See Pineapple Rule® Directions, pages 3-6.

BLOCK CORNERS/ROW 9: Stitch 3½″ squares together as shown. Press.

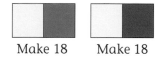

Make 18   Make 18

Use these for corners of blocks. See block diagram on page 30 for placement of color. To find center of Row 8, fold block in half and finger press a crease. Match crease to seam on 3½x6½″ rectangle.

2. ASSEMBLE: Place blocks as shown, rotating every other one to create red pinwheels and green pinwheels in alternate corners. Stitch blocks into horizontal rows. Stitch rows together. Press well.

3. BORDERS: Stitch Border 1 strips end to end using straight, not diagonal, seams. Press. Repeat with Border 2 strips and Border 3 strips. Cut 4 pieces 69″ long from each. Stitch Border 1, 2, and 3 pieces together. Press. Make 4. Pin one border to quilt, centered—there should be 12″ overlap at each end. Stitch, leaving seam allowance free at each end. Repeat on other 3 sides of quilt. Press mitered corners on ironing board as shown. Stitch. Trim seam allowance to ¼″ and press open.

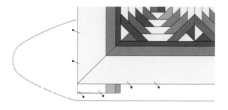

4. APPLIQUE: For vines, fuse web to wrong side of 12x20″ piece of vine fabric (green #1) and cut twenty ¼″ x 15″ **bias** strips. Arrange appliques using diagrams on page 54 and photo on page 31 as guides. Trim vine pieces to lengths needed while placing flowers and leaves, and hide ends of vine pieces under flowers. Stitch around appliques.

5. LAYER & QUILT: Piece backing to same size as batting. Layer and quilt as desired. Trim backing and batting even with quilt top.

6. BIND: Stitch binding strips end to end. Press in half lengthwise, wrong sides together. Bind quilt using ⅜″ seam allowance.

Poppies

Continued from page 32.

2. PANELS: Stitch blocks together with setting triangles, alternating reds and purples, as shown in diagram.

Left Panel
Make 1

Center Panel
Make 1

Right Panel
Make 1

3. ASSEMBLE & APPLIQUE: Measure panels and stitch black vertical sashing strips to that length. Make 2. Stitch panels and black vertical sashing pieces together as shown below. Press. For vines, fuse web to wrong side of 12 x 20″ piece of vine fabric and cut fourteen ⅜″ x 15″ **bias** strips. Trim vine pieces to lengths needed while placing poppies and leaves. Place poppies using photo on page 33 and diagram below as guides. Hide ends of vine pieces under other appliques. Stitch around appliques.

4. BORDER 1: Stitch pieces end to end for each side border. Press. Trim to fit sides of quilt. Stitch to quilt. Press. Repeat at top and bottom.

5. BORDER 2: Stitch strips together end to end using straight, not diagonal, seams. Press. Cut 2 pieces to fit sides of quilt. Stitch to quilt. Press. Repeat at top and bottom.

6. BORDER 3: From 2½″-wide purple strips, cut 2 pieces 38″ long for sides and 2 pieces 27″ long for top and bottom. Make 48 half-square triangle units. Press. Stitch triangle units and strips into borders as shown, adding purple squares to each end of top and bottom borders. Adjust length of purple pieces if necessary. Press. Stitch side borders to quilt. Press. Stitch top and bottom borders to quilt. Press.

■ Make 48

Sides - Make 2

Top & Bottom - Make 2

For each border, put sides on 1st, then top & bottom

7. BORDER 4: Repeat Step 5.

8. LAYER & QUILT: Piece backing vertically to same size as batting. Layer and quilt as desired. Trim backing and batting even with quilt top.

9. BIND: Stitch binding strips end to end. Press in half lengthwise, wrong sides together. Bind quilt using ⅜″ seam allowance.

Pineapple Pizzazz

Continued from page 34.

Lay Pineapple Rule® on wrong side of block, **inside diagonal lines on ruler on top of seam lines and center vertical line matching marked center line on center square.** A horizontal line on ruler may not fall exactly on the horizontal pencil line but should be parallel and equidistant from it. Trim the two triangles of fabric. Repeat on other corners.

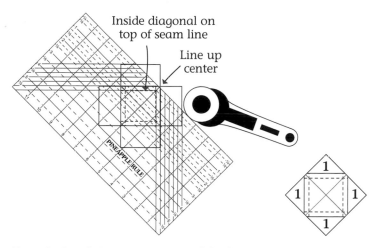

Inside diagonal on top of seam line

Line up center

Row 2: Stitch Row 2 pieces to block as in Row 1. They will be slightly longer than necessary. Press seam allowances to outside of block. Draw lines from corner to corner, keeping right angle at center. Lay ruler on block as before, **lining up the inside diagonal lines on the seam lines.** Continue to use center and horizontal lines on ruler. Trim corners.

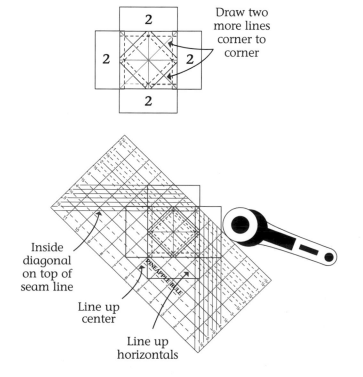

Draw two more lines corner to corner

Inside diagonal on top of seam line

Line up center

Line up horizontals

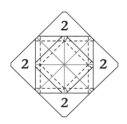

Row 3: Stitch Row 3 pieces to block. Press as before, being careful not to stretch the block. Lay ruler on block as before, **lining up the inside diagonal lines on the seam lines.** Continue to use center and horizontal lines on ruler. Trim corners.

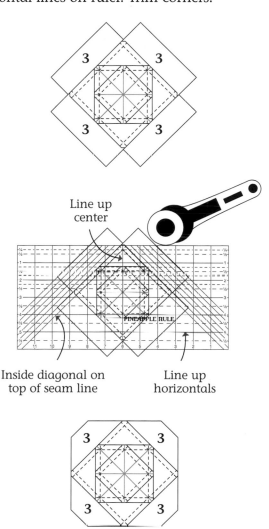

Line up center

Inside diagonal on top of seam line

Line up horizontals

HINT

To ensure accuracy, complete each row on all blocks as you go. Use the same ruler markings for each row on each block. The position of horizontal and diagonal lines will change as the blocks increase in size, but for each row, use the same set of lines.

Continued on page 52.

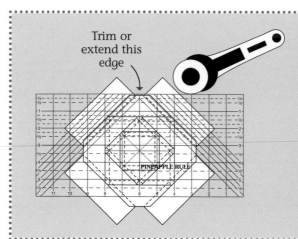

Trim or extend this edge

To match vertical, horizontal, and diagonal lines on ruler to block, you may need to trim or extend an edge. For example, you may have to move the ruler up or down, away from the edge of the previous row, in order to match the lines. This inaccuracy may be due to incorrect seam allowances, excessive pressing, stretching, etc. Trimming or extending an edge is a way to compensate so all blocks remain square and of equal size.

Row 4: Stitch Row 4 pieces to block. Press, being careful not to stretch the block. **Trim corners, this time lining up edge of ruler with edge of Row 3.** Continue to use center, horizontal, and diagonal guidelines on ruler.

Rows 5-9: Continue stitching and trimming in the same manner as for Row 4. To minimize distortion, sew with block on bottom, strip on top.

Rows 10-12 (corner): Stitch pieces for Rows 10-12 to corners of block (corners of block attach to Row 8). Press seam allowances toward outside of block. Line up one corner of the Pineapple Rule® with two adjacent sides of the block. Trim both sides of the corner without moving the ruler.

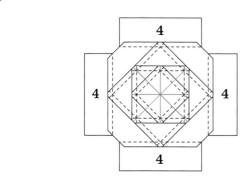

Line up edge of ruler with edge of Row 3

Line up diagonals

Line up Center

Line up horizontals

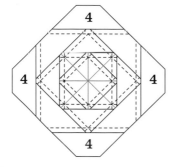

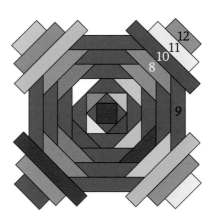

Assembly

1. **ASSEMBLE:** Stitch blocks into horizontal rows. Stitch rows together. Press well.

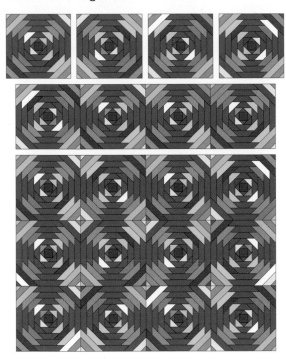

2. **BORDER 1:** Stitch side border strips together end to end with straight, not diagonal, seams. Cut 2 pieces to fit sides of quilt. Stitch to quilt. Press. Repeat at top and bottom with top/bottom border strips. Note: Side strips are narrower than top/bottom strips.

3. **BORDER 2:** Repeat Step 2. Strips are all the same width.

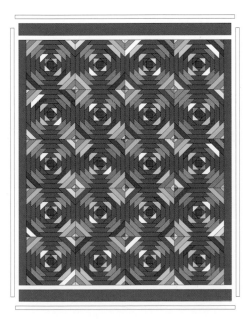

4. **BORDER 3:** For 2″ squares, stitch 2⅞″ black and white triangles together to make 136 half-square triangle units. For 1″ squares, stitch 1⅞″ black and white triangles together to make 272 half-square triangle units. Press. Stitch squares into 68 left-facing and 68 right-facing sections as shown. Press. Stitch sections into borders as shown. Press. Stitch side borders to quilt. Stitch top and bottom borders to quilt. If necessary, adjust seams between sections to make borders fit quilt. Press.

◣ 2″ squares - Make 136   ◣ 1″ squares - Make 272

◤ Left-facing Section - Make 68   ◥ Right-facing Section - Make 68

Side Border 3 - 38 Sections - Make 2

Top & Bottom Border 3 - 30 Sections - add squares to ends - Make 2

5. **BORDER 4:** Repeat Step 3.

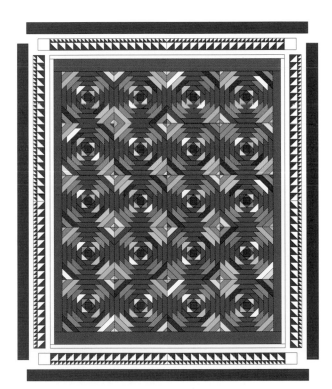

6. **LAYER & QUILT:** Piece backing vertically to same size as batting. Layer, baste, and quilt as desired.

7. **BIND:** Stitch binding strips end to end. Press in half lengthwise, wrong sides together. Bind quilt using ⅜″ seam allowance.

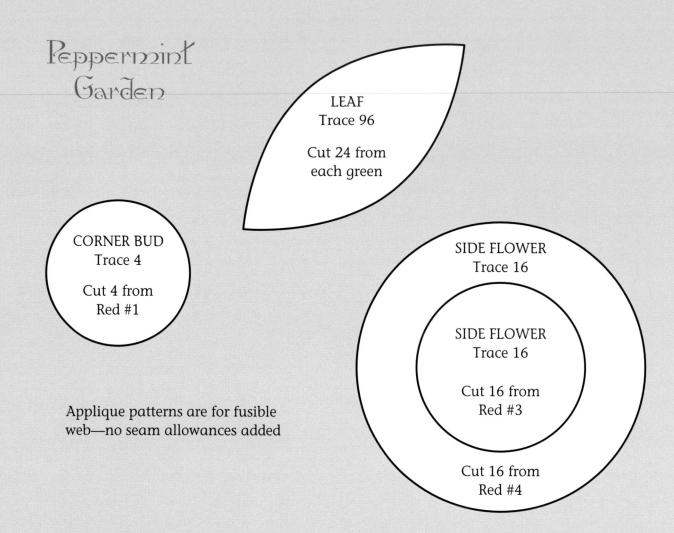

LEAF
Trace 96

Cut 24 from
each green

CORNER BUD
Trace 4

Cut 4 from
Red #1

SIDE FLOWER
Trace 16

SIDE FLOWER
Trace 16

Cut 16 from
Red #3

Cut 16 from
Red #4

Applique patterns are for fusible
web—no seam allowances added

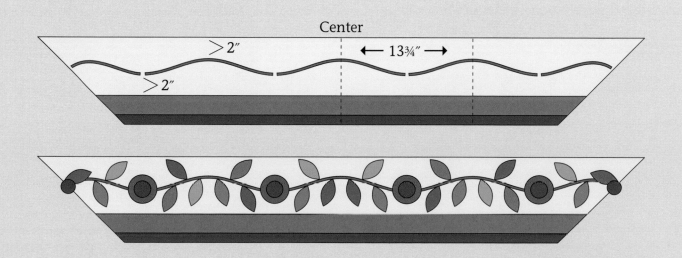

Center

> 2″

> 2″

← 13¾″ →

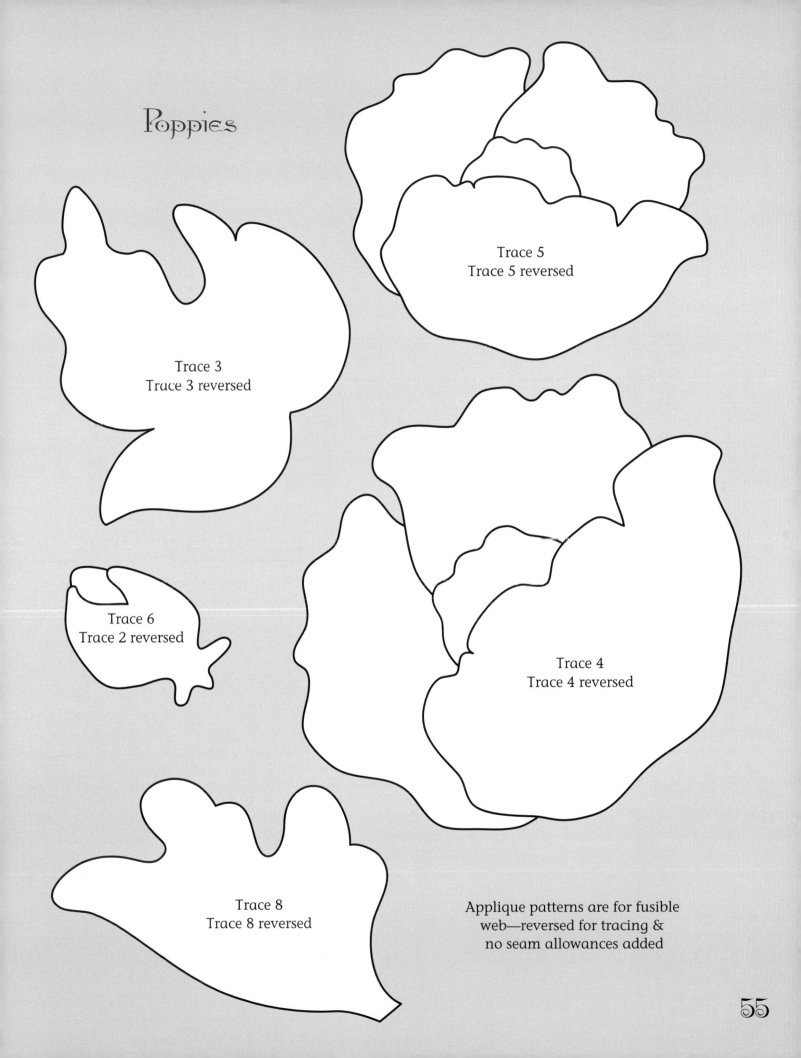

Poppies

Trace 5
Trace 5 reversed

Trace 3
Trace 3 reversed

Trace 6
Trace 2 reversed

Trace 4
Trace 4 reversed

Trace 8
Trace 8 reversed

Applique patterns are for fusible
web—reversed for tracing &
no seam allowances added

A Few More Possibilities

PINEAPPLE RULE®

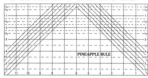

Special markings for making perfect Pineapples.
$11.00

Home for the Harvest
A Collection of Patchwork & Applique

Eighteen fall quilts & 20 small projects. Themes include back-to-school, Halloween & Thanksgiving.
$26.95

Divide &
Quilt it Your Way

Seventeen quilts to assemble using 4 different innovative "divide & conquer" techniques.
$25.95

Hearts Aplenty

Nineteen quilt patterns to warm your heart. Eight small bonus projects for you to make & share.
$26.95

Friends FOREVER
Quilting Together

Twenty quilts & wall hangings that celebrate friendship.
$26.95

Favorite Quilts

Favorite quilt patterns that can be made in five different sizes—from crib/wall to king size.
$19.95

P.S. I LOVE YOU THREE!

Twenty-one charming quilts for babies, toddlers & young children.
$22.95

Super Simple Squares
Creative Uses for 6½" Squares

Eighteen super simple quilts using packets of 6½" squares or strips.
$18.95

WELCOME TO MY CABIN

Cabin in the Woods quilt with 13 other projects that use elements taken from the main pattern.
$19.95

TOPPERS 2
Lynda Milligan & Nancy Smith

Fifteen different quilts to display on beds, couches, or tables.
$21.95

SUPER SIMPLE STRIPS
NANCY SMITH & LYNDA MILLIGAN

Eighteen fantastic quilts to create from precut 6½" strips or yardage.
$18.95

Home for the Holidays
Lynda Milligan & Nancy Smith

Twelve quilts & other projects that will wrap you in warmth & love for the holiday season.
$20.95

RED HOT ATTITUDE
Nancy Smith & Lynda Milligan

Five quilted wall hangings & many unique accessories to give to your friends.
$16.95

SUPER SIMPLE FAT QUARTER QUILTS
LYNDA MILLIGAN & NANCY SMITH

Patterns for 12 quilts using all those fat quarters you've been collecting.
$18.95

Seasonal Delights
NANCY SMITH & LYNDA MILLIGAN

Three cute seasonal quilts plus 6 other smaller quilts made from the same elements.
$19.95

POSSIBILITIES®

Fabric Designers for Avlyn, Inc. • Publishers of Possibilities® Books

Phone 303-740-6206 • Fax 303-220-7424 • Orders only U.S. & Canada 1-800-474-2665 • www.possibilitiesquilt.com